HAMZA GHAFAR

The Lion's Lament

Copyright © 2021 by Hamza Ghafar

All rights reserved. No part of this publication may be reproduced, stored or transmitted in any form or by any means, electronic, mechanical, photocopying, recording, scanning, or otherwise without written permission from the publisher. It is illegal to copy this book, post it to a website, or distribute it by any other means without permission.

First edition

Cover art by Bilaal Saleem

This book was professionally typeset on Reedsy. Find out more at reedsy.com

Contents

I   Allah, in whose name we begin, the Most Gracious, the Most Merciful

1	Foreword	3
2	Acknowledgements	12
3	Introduction	14
4	Chapter 1: Education	20
5	Poem 1: Simplicity or Greatness	30
6	Chapter 2: Wealth	31
7	Poem 2: Sky and Coast	40
8	Chapter 3: Friendship	41
9	Poem 3: Pain is the Answer	47
10	Chapter 4: Happiness	48
11	Poem 4: Life is a Melody	57
12	Chapter 5: Discipline	58
13	Poem 5: Ambition	63
14	Chapter 6: Manhood and Womanhood	64
15	Poem 6: Love God	70
16	Chapter 7: Arrogance	71
17	Poem 7: Passage of Time	74
18	Chapter 8: Truth	75
19	Poem 8: Fly or Fall	76
20	Chapter 9: Love	77

21	Chapter 10: Parting Words	78
22	Bibliography	86

I

Allah, in whose name we begin, the Most Gracious, the Most Merciful

"Verily, among the best of you are those with the best character." (Bukhari and Muslim)

"I have been sent to perfect good character." (Al-Muwatta)

- The Prophet Muhammad (peace and blessings of Allah be upon him)

1

Foreword

The intention behind this work is to record some reflections on experiences of mine on what I believe to be some of the key components of life. These understandings are influenced by several sources, first and foremost being my Religion (Islam), and then, to name a few, the likes of Marcus Garvey, Malcolm X, Muhammad Ali, Mawlana Rumi and many other people and ideas. I agree with some and disagree with others but gained inspiration and understanding from them all. And ultimately Allah Almighty is the Source.

I begin this task at the age of 18. I will continue to learn more and be inspired by different views and people as I mature. As I age, so will the book. There may be evidence of shifts in the style of delivery, possibly even contradictions due to my views altering, in which case I hope I will make it clear that a previous view I held or mentioned in the book is no longer what I hold. I want to allow the possibility of showing in my writing organic growth – through the writing itself in terms of my expression either getting better or worse (hopefully not the latter), as well as maybe through a change of opinion on certain things. Such growth is what living is all about. However, this depends on how long this task will take me, which itself depends on how much I want to write. Most likely it will be short, so maybe this won't happen. Oh well, it was a nice sentiment. I also want to show that you can busy yourself with what shall proceed in the book whilst also focusing on other commitments, be it one's education or early career. At my age it may be the case that young men and women are omitting spending time evaluating things like the reality of friendship, truth and so on in order to focus on building a career. I'd argue that realising these points will aid in achieving one's goals. Therefore, they shouldn't be ignored in favour of other matters.

The earlier we focus on self-reflection and the significant points the book will reference, the better prepared we shall be for achieving our targets. For me, however, such reflections weren't for, nor are they in order to achieve, some sort of worldly goal. That is an extra bonus so to speak, which is a result of the fact that these things are from the Qur'an and the example of the Prophet peace be upon him; the Qur'an and the Sunnah give us guidance of how to handle our affairs in this world. Nevertheless, it was due to a focus on the Hereafter, the Akhirah, that I spent time reflecting on such matters. Indeed, we have a Lord who we shall be held accountable to. He will ask us of our Prayer and Charity, but also of our dealings with the world, with people. He will ask us of how we were with ourselves, as well – how we nourished our bodies and minds and hearts. This reality is what motivates me, despite my weakness in being disciplined enough to refrain from that which would displease the Lord. May He forgive me.

During proof-reading, I decided to add this to the foreword: I've set myself a target that I will publish this work around the time I turn twenty-one and no later than twenty-two. Sultan Mehmet Fatih "the Conqueror" conquered Constantinople, the seat of the Byzantine Empire that survived so many sieges giving it a reputation of being almost impossible to take, when he was twenty-one. Muhammad Ali became the World Heavyweight Champion defeating the then unbeatable Sonny Liston at the age of twenty-two; Mike Tyson became World Heavyweight Champion at twenty. I looked at these men who I grew up admiring and noted how incredibly hard they worked. Their work ethic caused them to achieve so much at apparently such a young age. I looked to myself and asked: "what have you achieved?"

This reminds me of the story of Julius Caesar when he was in his early 30's, who, after looking upon a statue of Alexander the Great, began to weep. When asked why he cries at the sight of the stone face of Alexander, he said how Alexander in his twenties had conquered the known-world and stamped his name everywhere, and died at 32/33 with such a legacy. Yet Caesar stood at 33 having achieved no memorable feat of his own.

I am sitting here, age twenty on the 28th of February 2019. I shall turn twenty-one on the 25th of July. Around that time, I hope to have self-published this work as the first of however many I end up writing in the future. I am in my second year of university. The bulk of the writing began during my first year. I imagine I could have finished this quickly but haven't been able to sit and write anything for longer than fifteen or twenty minutes, due to all my other commitments that take up most of my time. At points I went a few months without even opening the document. Sometimes I'd only add one single sentence and then proceed to not add anything for another month or two. This did allow me to experience and reflect more, so in-fact aided my work. Had I rushed, the work wouldn't have been as complete. At the same time, however, I didn't want to keep delaying.

I'm back again, editing. It is the 22nd of August, 2021 and I'm 23 haha. I've realised that we like to feel good about ourselves so we do and say things that aren't always rooted completely in reality. I mentioned Caesar and Alexander. In fact, I now say they achieved naught, and this goes for everyone, if they failed/fail to seek their Lord. A much better example to use would be that of the great companion of the Prophet (peace be upon him), Sa'ad ibn Mu'adh. A companion who accepted Islam at the age of 30/31, and passed away at the age of 36/37. Yet, upon his passing, it is narrated that the Throne (Arsh) of Allah shook for him, such was his rank (Bukhari). He achieved that with 6/7 years of service. Not because he studied and received multiple degrees or became a multi-millionaire, but because he loved God and the Prophet (peace be upon him) immensely. What are the cheers of humans as compared to the shaking of the Throne?! Another companion, Usama bin Zayd was as young as 17, and some say in his early 20's, when he was appointed as commander of the Muslim armies for a Syrian expedition by the Prophet (peace be upon him) – leading the likes of Abu Bakr, Umar, Ali and Uthman (God be well pleased with them all).

All the people I have looked up to as a child and growing up (like the ones mentioned), especially the ultimate example being the Prophet Muhammad (upon whom be peace), have all served mankind in whatever way they could. As Muhammad Ali said: "service to others is the rent you pay for your room here on Earth." This is my attempt to try and pay my rent. I hope it isn't my only attempt, either. I was also asked by several people to write, so I thought "why not?". Since I was a child, writing has always been something I enjoyed. Now I do what I enjoy with the hope of achieving something good. Win-win situation for me. Though I strongly believe that before you try to help others, you must first help yourself. As Rumi said: "yesterday I was clever, so I wanted to change the world. Today I am wise, so I change myself." It is mentioned in the Qur'an that "Indeed, Allah will not change the condition of a people until they change what is in themselves." (Qur'an 13:11) In order to bring about change, one must first change. I look at the lack of years I possess, the lack of knowledge and experience, and deficiency in upright character and realise I should not be attempting something I am not worthy of nor capable of doing. Put simply, I'm not in the position to try and help others. Yet, if not me, then who? I wish success upon those who are attempting to do good.

My main goal behind this book is to bring about some sort of awareness literally just in my town amongst those of a similar heritage. However, I also know that what I write about are universal principles that can be applied to any type of person, because I learnt some of these from Jamaican Christians like Marcus Garvey, ancient Chinese generals like Sun Tzu, political thinkers of the Renaissance like Machiavelli, Martial Artists like Bruce Lee and sports' greats like LeBron James. As a hadith mentions: "the word of wisdom is the lost property of the believer. Wherever he finds it, he is most deserving of it" (Tirmidhi). As I get older, it is becoming more and more clear to me that the Qur'an and Sunnah have addressed everything. I didn't need LeBron James to show me the importance and benefit of looking after one's body. In-fact, if it wasn't for the fact that the Qur'an and Sunnah teach and recommend it, and the narrations about the physical strength of the Prophet (peace be upon him), LeBron James may not have even appealed to me. At least that's how I hope and want to think.

What's my point here? These things are just things to be enjoyed, otherwise can be distractions to the reality. It sounds nice and smart to be able to quote many different philosophers and thinkers and this and that, but it's all folly at the end of it. There is a hadith concerning the End of Times, that religious ignorance shall prevail (Bukhari). This refers to the lack of knowledge of the Hereafter and that which concerns it – the Qur'an and Sunnah. In this day and age, we Muslims like to get knowledge from everywhere except the Qur'an and Sunnah, in order to feel accomplished – myself included. A knowledge that makes us haughty. Whereas knowledge of Qur'an and Sunnah humbles one the more he/she learns, if done sincerely.

I'm no historian or academic. I haven't the understanding of the ideas of these individuals or their lives and experiences to that calibre. Nonetheless, from what little I have read and come to learn so far, I've gained some insight to write. If I was able to gain this understanding, then you can, too. That's probably the main point I want to put across: it doesn't take a genius to understand these principles because I certainly am not one. Other than this, I merely want to encourage thought on important matters. Once the mind is engaged in beneficial matters, the picture shall draw itself with the permission of God Almighty. Ultimately, guidance and knowledge are a light and blessing from God. The Prophet (peace be upon him) said, "Allah says: 'I am just as My slave thinks I am, (i.e. I am able to do for him what he thinks I can do for him) and I am with him if He remembers Me. If he remembers Me in himself, I too, remember him in Myself; and if he remembers Me in a group of people, I remember him in a group that is better than they; and if he comes one span nearer to Me, I go one cubit nearer to him; and if he comes one cubit nearer to Me, I go a distance of two outstretched arms nearer to him; and if he comes to Me walking, I go to him running'" (Bukhari). Take the step, plant the seed, and God shall do the rest and what is best.

Neither am I an authority on Islam. I pray that God forgives any mistakes I may have made in this work or in my understanding. This in itself is a beautiful lesson from Islam – that we are fallible beings who shouldn't shy away from being at fault.

We should instead turn to Allah in repentance, which indeed brings us closer to Him. Practising Islam has increasingly been stigmatised, from my experience, into some sort of puritan, joyless, strict existence where you have to be sinless to be regarded as a real Muslim. This is so far from the reality. This thinking alienates many, who will then seek to fill the void in their hearts with something else and ending up in a vicious cycle as a result. Islam is for one and all. We should be working towards making our youth people of Salah and lovers of their religion, not to force unrealistic expectations of perfection upon them. Hence why I feel it is important for sinners (like myself) who, despite their short-comings, value Islam to speak (within bounds). Indeed, we should all be aiming for perfection, but with the understanding that we are anything but perfect...

Though this is a small work, this shouldn't be read in haste. Take your time reading each chapter. Indeed, read them multiple times before moving to the next. Reflect and try to understand. Discuss what you read with your families. Ask your friends' their opinion and begin a beneficial conversation.

Do not take what I say on board without thought, no matter how nice it sounds. I am merely writing what I feel is correct, based on what I have learned and experienced. It may not apply to you in the slightest because of your own experiences and your own learning. Perhaps it will only make sense with time. You may also feel that I am completely incorrect. This is fine.

In between each chapter, acting as separators, I've added some poems I have come up with. They're written in a sonnet form. They do not have titles, and are on different topics/feelings. I hope you enjoy them.

2

Acknowledgements

I must mention my parents. Whatever goodness I have cultivated in myself and spread, and hopefully will further enhance, is the result of my parents' wisdom, love, prayers and guidance. I believe I inherited my love of literature, poetry, history and the Arts from them. The simplest people I know, yet the wisest. May God bless them with all that is good and save them from all that is bad.

I extend my thanks to every single teacher I have ever had, from my school teachers to all of my Madrassah teachers. My words of appreciation cannot express my gratitude sufficiently. God will reward you for your goodness.

Finally, I thank my friends who have supported me in this endeavour, particularly brother Danyal Ahmed Khalik who proof-read the work and provided constructive feedback, and brother Bilaal Saleem for the cover design.

ACKNOWLEDGEMENTS

"...my guidance is only from Allah; I rely upon Him and towards Him only do I incline." (Quran, 11:88)

3

Introduction

To think that life is easy, or will become easy, is a dangerous mindset. The man or woman in the mansion can be facing just as much struggle as the man or woman living on the street, though the struggle takes a different shape. It's also important, however, to appreciate that there are struggles more difficult than others. Nevertheless, a degree, financial stability or a big house will not grant access to an easy life. Life is a constant up and down journey, and absolutely every single person will face struggles. This is a fact that cannot be avoided. Just as death is inevitable, so is coming face to face with difficulty.

Money will not resolve your bad relationships. A great degree cannot mend your broken heart. Simply becoming a lawyer will not give you peace of mind. At times we can go to great lengths to try and fix something in our life but to no avail. You must understand: something broken can be fixed, but that which takes a whole new shape can't be reversed into its old form. You have to adapt. This ultimately means that our happiness can't be subject to something that can and/or will change. For example, if I tell myself that I can only be happy if I am rich, does that mean I live my life in sadness until I reach the point of becoming financial wealthy (which usually means having more money than you can spend)? What about if, after gaining it, something happens, and I lose a lot of money - is my happiness to go along with it? Depending on temporary things will make my happiness just that - temporary. Therefore, seek it in the Eternal (which I believe is God). So shall be your happiness. It is also about possessing certain qualities that I found in believing in Islam as a way of life, which is to be content with whatever you have, being hopeful for what is to come (in this world and in Heaven most importantly) and possessing patience and gratitude. Not wanting much in the form of luxuries and belongings but being grateful for everything is the simplest recipe for a peaceful mind.

That being said, it doesn't mean sadness will never be experienced; one can only truly appreciate happiness when sadness is felt. It shouldn't be something we try to run away from. Embrace it. Just don't let it squeeze the life from you. Understanding that this life is a test, and is supposed to be difficult at times, is important. Therefore revise. Study. Learn the skills, gather the knowledge required to manoeuvre through the struggles so that we may pass, so that we may triumph. When you study for a test, as difficult as the questions may be, having learnt beforehand allows you to give an answer of some kind... and I prefer that to having to sit on my hands, dumb. Life is the same. Learning is a requirement for obtaining the answers to deal with the difficulties that await.

The world is a crazy place. Many atrocities and evils happen on a daily basis. Despite the constant sorrow and heartbreak, there are so many beauties. However, seeing only the joys of life is a disrespect towards the suffering and sadness, while focusing only on the sadness brings people down into the same abyss. It's all about balance. Seek happiness, and aim to spread it also. As I get older, I am seeing more and more selfishness. I am seeing less care, less love, less empathy. I especially worry for those younger than me. They are so absorbed in money and games and technology; they don't seem to know of much else. Of-course, they can't be entirely blamed for this, for it is the direction the world has taken. We are conditioned by our environment. But the world isn't only just that. They should be shown alternatives, and that life is more than just haircuts, designer clothing and acting tough (the youngsters from where I'm from, at least). Then there are those who only have a persona online, and in real life don't have basic manners and etiquette. The elders have forgotten their roots and principles in pursuit of a "good life" here in this country, leaving their children without knowledge of who they are and where they come from. Those children are then susceptible to a system which thrives on making people believe money is the answer, rather than the Qur'an, or Salah, or helping others.

Growing up, my parents have never ever told me to aim for riches. They've never told me to get the best grades or work hard so that I can get a high paying job to make an easy life for myself. I've always been taught that life is always going to have struggles and difficulties, "so son, become educated." Learn. Make yourself a good and strong person so that you can handle what life throws at you and help those around you. I've been taught to work hard to become the best person I can be. Today, regardless of how a bad person is, if he/she has a lot of money, they're automatically successful and should be followed it seems.

Money should not be the only measure of one's respect and success. How someone earns it, a man or woman's work ethic, is what deserves to be respected. Otherwise only the rich will be the recipients of love and respect, whereas those who work extremely hard but only earn little are looked down upon purely because they possess less material or don't do a more glamorous job. This isn't fair.

At the same time, however, there are clearly elements of transition. There is a rising awareness amongst the youth regarding mental health, diet and fitness, and political realities; pro-activity amongst young women in seeking knowledge and trying to figure out how best to navigate the current atmosphere, and a large spectrum of interests being sought, from sports to more artistic ventures – things that perhaps had a specific stigma attached to them in our culture (though this wasn't the case historically). These are now being challenged, to a degree. However, as much as there is potential for positive change in this, it could become a recipe for disaster should this transition fail to be ushered towards the right direction with the correct understanding. We must evaluate: to what end are these changes being made?

We must seek to improve under the guiding light of Islam, not anything else. The very struggles our culture has faced – whether it be dishonouring and degrading women, to the lack of awareness surrounding mental health issues or an abandonment and lack of appreciation for the arts is a result of leaving our Islamic heritage. Where it was Muslim women to open the first University in the world, we now see girls being kept away from studying; where we had figures like Mawlana Rumi, Mawlana Jaami, Mian Muhammad Bakhsh and Allama Iqbal leading the way in poetry, it is a pursuit looked down upon or attached with a specific stigma so that boys and men avoid it.

Rather than going on a whole tangent in this introduction, I'll sum up what I'm trying to say: we have to re-evaluate our entire mindset if we, as a community and people, are to progress. There is too much hatred, jealousy, selfishness, ignorance and prejudice; it's holding us back in this life, and we have God to answer to in the Next Life. We must encourage both individuality and brotherhood/sisterhood. We must embrace good character. We must grasp knowledge. We must love more. We must understand what we were and how we've fallen so that we may rise once again. The state of Muslims around the world is proof that we, as a people, have clearly veered from the right path. How have we the audacity to speak of success, individually and otherwise, when we are in such a state? We are, in-fact, delusional. Not successful. It is irrelevant how much money or how many qualifications you have, when you're losing everything else. The words of Sayyiduna Umar (Allah be pleased with him) suffice in this context: "We were the most humiliated people on earth and Allah gave us honour through Islam. If we ever seek honour through anything else, Allah will humiliate us again (Hakim)."

4

Chapter 1: Education

Probably the aspect of life that is incredibly watered-down as well as over-emphasised at my age. What do I mean by this? All ages, be it a child or a senior, are made to feel that without the so-called 'education' provided, we cannot achieve much. This is due to a system that promotes this for its own agendas. I am 18. I see it and hear it day by day, the stress of my friends and relatives over such matters. "I need these qualifications, so I can get a good paying job, in order to live comfortably."

Money. Whether we admit it or not, whether we acknowledge it or not, whether we are even aware of it or not, the pursuit of 'education' and grades is for just that one thing: money. Generally. I will not paint the brush over everyone. But the society we live in dictates that the 'successful' are those with huge amounts of wealth. This has created an institutionalised and formalised materialistic mindset within the walls of education. As a result, I personally feel youth are not in touch with history (their own especially), and do not empathise or 'feel' the way even our grandparents would, because we've become so caught up in this endless pursuit for big bank accounts. We don't pay attention to much else. Online (on social media) we are bombarded with luxury lifestyles; in school we are drilled with career paths; at home, our parents are screaming to study hard to procure a good job; your friends speak only about designer clothes and obsess over drug dealers who drive nice cars. Who's talking about the importance of good manners? It's not just that we fail to pay attention to anything else, we're hardly presented anything else! Yes, money is also a means of helping others but not the only way. Think about the hundreds of charities that exist - if money was truly helping the way it is said to help, poverty would be wiped out by now. Money alone isn't going to solve the problem. Wanting to use it in the right way is necessary and that will only come with being brought up with the desire to give and share, rather than only being conditioned to take and keep.

Education should be for the enhancement of human character, ability and potential in order to benefit oneself and others around him/her - physically, mentally and spiritually. How to honourably earn a living is part of this. Imam Ghazali mentions in his famous Mukhtasar Ihya Ulum ad-Din that the Prophet (peace be upon him) said: "The most useful of people is the knowledgeable who, when needed, imparts knowledge, and when not needed, enriches himself with it" (ibn Majah); "the nearest people to the rank of Prophethood are the people of knowledge… because they guide people to what the Prophets bring" (Ahmed) which is to live in accordance with God's guidance – and God desires we live moral, just lives. Hence, education should ultimately be for the purpose of attaining goodness in character. What may fall in between, such as respect, wealth and fame as a result of attaining knowledge and becoming, for example, a doctor, are extra perks and enjoyments. But do not let those enjoyments make you lose sight of the bigger goal – improving yourself and your environment. The scholars in Islam (Ulema) are so revered (and are the ones referred to in the statements of the Prophet) because they are the foremost in knowledge, in its practise and in spreading it. They please God. Not because they are millionaire geniuses. The scholars who do gain riches use it to build schools, places of worship, sponsor poorer children's educations and so on. They do not simply indulge in luxury.

Imam Ghazali goes on to state that 'whoever lacks knowledge has a sick heart, and its demise is a certainty. He does not feel it, because the distractions of the world numb his senses. When, however, death lifts the veil of those distractions, the senses return, and great pain is felt, together with endless regret.'

The knowledge Imam Ghazali refers to is beneficial knowledge, which for Muslims is whatever increases one in awareness of God, and makes us better equipped to deal with the issues affecting humanity. Imagine, then, seeking 'education' or 'knowledge' purely for the world (wealth, luxuries and comfort), which is numbing us! The Imam's statement shows that knowledge is in-fact supposed to help us see beyond our bellies, not only help us fill it. You can learn all you want, but if your goal remains selfish and worldly, you've in actuality learned naught. Knowledge must be linked to a greater purpose and followed by action.

We are killing our hearts and are at the same time numbing ourselves from the pain. We remain heedless to our hearts' deaths by chasing all this money, these cars, these high paying jobs, purely for the sake of possessing them to delude ourselves into thinking we've reached success. We must ask ourselves: whose definition of success are we living by? The success dictated to us by a godless, confused society that can't even decide what is right and wrong? Or the success in accordance to what Musa, Eesa and Muhammad (peace be upon them all) have taught?

Getting good grades isn't bad. Having a great job isn't bad. But doing it all for basically nothing *is*. Achieve them for the correct reason… You can live a life that you enjoy whilst still doing your duty to God and to humanity. You can have a big house and a nice car. Just do not assume that that is success. It is merely an enjoyment. "What is the life of this world but play and amusement? But best is the home in the hereafter, for those who are righteous. Will ye not then understand?" (Qur'an, 6:32)"

Education isn't and shouldn't be for money exclusively. Education covers absolutely everything, including how to make money. If you're trying to get your degree just so you can get a high-paying job, however, you need to re-evaluate. But for whatever reason, that's something that isn't really taught in schools and colleges. They teach the curriculum, but don't say why we should be learning all these things. Instead, we are only shown career paths and job options and Universities. Not with the fact that ultimately this should all be for self-improvement, and then to improve the world around us - using the skills, knowledge and wealth we gain from learning. This is why I find 'Education' (referring to the schooling system) watered-down whilst at the same time over-emphasised above real learning. Don't believe me? Why don't schools teach students about financing, how to invest, how to use wealth? Schools prepare us to be future employees of established, rich institutions. That's it. They're making robots. They keep you following orders, following mark schemes, and thinking within constraints.

Don't think that schooling is enough. Learn for yourself. Read. Do well in school/university, but don't remain within that boundary. Study more. Study history outside of what they teach, read books outside of what they give you. It's just common sense anyway; the schools, colleges and universities can only teach so much (plus, they'll only teach within a certain light). Why restrain yourself? I'll tell you why: because that's all we need to get a job. Back to money it seems… Thankfully, I was fortunate enough to have teachers who understood this, and valued good character just as much as they valued good marks in a test. Teachers don't have much choice in the matter, sadly. They have a job to do in order to earn a living. They have to teach the materials they are given, so don't be hard on them. If there's anyone you want to be annoyed at about the watered-down education you're receiving, be annoyed at the system.

We can still attend secular/non-religious schools who of-course do not possess this spiritual or religious type of understanding – but that doesn't mean we as a result should forsake our spiritual and religious understanding. They are not mutually exclusive. You can continue studying everything you normally study in schools. That's not the issue. The issue is the purpose. The intention behind it. The schools may not delve into these topics, but it doesn't matter because Islam does. Take your learning into your own hands.

But what's the danger of such thinking? What's wrong with pursuing money? I want to focus on this point in more detail later in the book, but briefly: the turmoil we are currently witnessing in the world today is a result of the rich wanting to become richer – a world built on greed. The system we live in wants us to continuously chase wealth and work tirelessly to do so because it makes the rich even richer. You gain a tiny fraction, though you're the one doing all the work. It's a facade. Earn your money, of-course. You have to. You have to contribute to society. Just understand that it's a game and you're being played. Therefore, there's no point making it your goal. Money is a means, albeit to very important things like building orphanages, hospitals and so on. You should be aiming to get a high-paying job so that you can perform such deeds! Not so you can call yourself a millionaire. The focus should be trying to earn money in a positive manner that doesn't require you to lose your health or happiness, and earn in a way that can help your communities.

Chase your passion, not money. In chasing what you enjoy and are born to do, you earn a living and happiness, whereas if you only chase money, you may have to give up your joy. As Muslims, we should have a firm belief in the provision that God has written for us: if you're going to be a millionaire, nothing can stop that from happening. So just relax, and worry yourself with reaching those millions in a good way rather than trying to take short-cuts, lie and deceive, or (as is popular in our community) by becoming a low-life drug dealer who destroys families and communities just to buy a nice car before reaching twenty-five years old.

Ignorance is the greatest cancer. Cut this tumour out as soon as possible. It only creates negativity. Remaining within the constraints of schooling will not do the job. We have to learn more. The reality is that this cancer is a death-sentence: we are born ignorant, and shall die so. But that doesn't mean we suffer throughout. We need to tame the illness. Calm the symptoms. At least then we can die somewhat peacefully... And what are the symptoms of this disease? Greed, racism, negativity and so on. Only in the pursuit of knowledge is it possible for these symptoms to be removed. So, work hard and focus. And remember that life is vast. Don't limit yourselves to grades. Yes, they open doors, but it's not like those are the only doors. If you rely on those few letters to achieve something, that only proves you have not been educated at all.

CHAPTER 1: EDUCATION

Sun Tzu in the famous work "The Art of War" states: 'If you know the enemy and know yourself, you need not fear the result of a hundred battles. If you know yourself but not the enemy, for every victory gained you will also suffer a defeat. If you know neither the enemy nor yourself, you will succumb in every battle.' Though a treatise on warfare, the principles in Sun Tzu's "Art of War" are very much applicable to everyday life - if one interprets them in that light. For me personally, the 'battles' are the many different types of battles in life that a person will face: difficulty in relationships/friendships, struggles in the exam room or hardship in the workplace…

In order to know yourself, you must first understand that there is actually a need for such an awareness. Here's a thought for you: if you don't even know your own self, what makes you think you will ever learn about others? Whether you're surrounded by real or fake people? You can't gauge your potential until you analyse who and what you are. Neglecting this journey will cause a person to pass by life as merely a shell of what he or she is supposed to become. Your job here is to evolve into the best person you can possibly be. Before an artist, a mechanic, a scientist or a physician gets to work, he/she first familiarises himself/herself with the tools; before you can begin working to become the best person you can be you must first become familiar with what you're working with i.e. yourself. Embark upon this road and notice how life becomes a less daunting thing. You'll see everything as a means to realising your own greatness. This leaves you feeling content, for your only concern becomes self-improvement. You become free.

As for knowing your enemy, that I shall tell you. In Arabic, he is called "Shaytaan". In English, "Satan". For those who may not believe in religion or God, then I will say "Evil", "Injustice", "Immorality", though one wonders where do these understandings come from if not stemming from a belief in God. Your enemy is also your own self: your weaknesses, your carnal self. This again shows the importance of traversing your own person, for within you lie not just Your Friend, but your enemy.

Rumi states that the art of knowing is knowing what to ignore. There is beneficial knowledge, and knowledge of no benefit. How can we decide which is which? As Muslims, our scholars have mentioned clearly that beneficial knowledge is whatever increases your Taqwa, awareness of God. Whatever makes you forget Him is of no benefit, but in-fact harmful. If you keep the Hereafter and God at the forefront of your mind, many of your actions and pursuits which seem 'regular' or just a part of day-to-day activities become the foundation to building your here-after. For example: aim for the great job and to earn wealth so that you can help God's creation, so that you can aid the poor, so that you can battle the ills of society. You're getting what you want (I.e. a great job and money) whilst also doing what God wants, which is to do good works. It's a win-win situation.

God doesn't expect you to give away all of your wealth. Imagine if we all just gave our Zakat properly. We'd keep the vast majority of our wealth to use for our enjoyment, whilst fulfilling our duty to God and society... 'Do they not reflect in their own minds?' (Qur'an, 30:8). Indeed, the best education is education which benefits yourself and others. You cannot benefit nor educate others without first educating and benefiting yourself, and you cannot benefit nor educate yourself without benefiting and educating others. This is the ultimate journey of life. It is once we dedicate ourselves to this that we shall be able to feel free and feel true happiness. May this all serve as a reminder to myself, first.

5

Poem 1: Simplicity or Greatness

Simplicity or greatness – my choices.
Yet in simplicity I see beauty;
Shyness in greats, so I ignore voices
Pulling me to their desires cruelly.

The reigns are in my hands exclusively
While God creates the roads and the pathways.
I'm stumbling, or rising allusively
As I navigate this difficult maze.

At times nothing seems to makes sense to me.
This is the mind's end, and where the spirit
Should lead. It wants to go to God's decree.
Eyes locked, heart on the goal of no limit.

We're not here for long, friend, so take heed.
Seek good, and spread good, and you will be freed.

6

Chapter 2: Wealth

You're rich if you're happy. You'll find there are millionaires that depend on drink and drugs because they don't feel happy despite living in luxury. Money itself doesn't bring peace of mind. That only comes from being content. Happiness comes from loving and being loved. Take away your family and your friends who you care for and exchange them for millions of pounds. Would you feel happy? This might all sound cliché and I am cringing as I type this, but it's the reality. Happiness is a mindset. Not a material thing. Everything here has the capability to make you feel very good but also extremely sad, be it money, family, your friends - you name it. Remaining happy, however, requires a development from within so that when, for example, a parent passes away, or you're low on funds, or your friend does something to hurt you, you're able to move quickly away from the sadness or, in some cases, not even be affected. Don't let things mess up your vibe.

On the flip side, however, a source of stress is also lack of money.

My mum would remind my siblings and I regularly that people are always facing something, regardless of who they are, or what their position in life. Some have all the wealth and luxury, but battle loneliness, or a family crisis. Then there are those who've a good family life but lack financial stability. The rich in this circumstance wish for the family system of the poor (for example), while the poor wish to have the wealth of the rich. Such is the enigma of life. That's why, again, it's important to try and find happiness within ourselves so that we can still feel good because there's always something that we're going to have to face, and others will always possess something that we think we are missing. External sources such as financial stability, or a nice holiday, or a good grade are a means of increasing happiness, or keeping at bay large difficulties – not creating it (happiness). To create happiness, you must look to yourself. It's also important to remember, however, that people are different. What increases my happiness may differ from you. Playing football might do it for me; going on a shopping spree for you. But you won't always get what you want. Your job is to remain smiling despite that, otherwise life will become too unbearable.

However, it's dangerous to fall into the trap of romanticising poverty, that they somehow are more "real" humans who may not have money but have love, and family and so on. This may be the case sometimes, but not all the time of-course. If rich people sitting in their beautiful homes can suffer from mental health issues and feel suicidal, imagine what the homeless person is going through. Imagine the mental health problems a young boy in the ghetto is facing having to witness shootings and murders and drugs regularly. It should be no surprise when such a child grows up violent, unhappy and angry. That is why Islam focuses so much on not hoarding wealth but investing back into the community and giving in charity/zakat - to combat conditions that create crime and anger. It's known that poorer communities end up turning to things like drink and drug in order to cope with the difficulties – creating a bigger difficulty instead.

Rather than saying money doesn't bring about happiness, I think it may be better to say that materialism doesn't. Money is just a means. It can become a source of increasing happiness, though it can't create it, as mentioned. Materialism and luxury bring about enjoyment, but it's fleeting. You buy one pair of new shoes, and you'll be pleased with them until the new design is released a few months later. Now your eyes are on the new shoes. Materialism is a business built on a cycle of short-term satisfaction and constant desire for the next new thing. As the Prophet (peace be upon him) said: "If Adam's son had a valley full of gold, he would like to have two valleys, for nothing fills his mouth except dust. And Allah forgives him who repents to Him" (Bukhari and Muslim). Chase materialism and wealth all you want; it'll never satisfy you. At the end of it all, when we shall lay in our deathbeds, what we will desire most is to be surrounded by people who we loved, and loved us in return. What we will recall is fond memories with them. We will look back on what we are leaving behind. Is it going to be a life of service to people that remains as our legacy, or a life of serving only oneself? The latter shall lead to a very lonely death… you can't hear reassuring words from money.

I should mention that sometimes, we have to delay our dreams and chasing our passion (something I mentioned in the previous chapter) in order to earn money – and this is reality. We must sometimes bite the bullet and work where we don't like to in order to earn for ourselves and families, and that is strength. That is putting duty before yourself, which is something I will explore later.

You're especially rich if you have knowledge. Wisdom. Rich in character and heart. This is the true wealth. My father said to me once: "Son, if money is such a treasure and the mark of being truly wealthy, drug dealers and criminals have money. Lots of it. Is that wealth? Real wealth is the respect you have." How you treat others (well), and how they respect and admire you – this is real wealth. And (real) respect is only gained from respectful people.

Money is very important, but I have an issue with this culture of money hoarding, trying to gather as much as you possibly can – above what you need – in order to feel like you have achieved something. To feel success. There's nothing wrong with getting a high paying job. But what are you going to do with that money? Keep it for yourself/spend on yourself just to feel special? Then you're not wealthy. You're greedy. If you used that money to fulfil your needs, your family's needs, and gave in charity, then you are wealthy. Then you've used money as it should be used.

CHAPTER 2: WEALTH

The Prophet (peace be upon him) didn't live in a palace. He slept on the floor. He would go days without food. He didn't carry bags of gold on him wherever he went – he carried a miswak (natural toothbrush) instead. Whatever money he would attain, he would give away in charity. His friends described him as living very simply, but when it came to giving (in charity), he would put a King to shame. Peace be upon him. That's how you use wealth. To uplift the community, because then you shall reap rewards far greater than what short-term pleasure materialism promises. You'll garner love and earn respect; you'll be making the world a better place in some form, earning the prayers of many. Ultimately, and most importantly, you'll be pleasing The Almighty, which should be our primary aim. It should serve as an eye opener for us Muslims of today that our Prophet peace be upon him said that the poor shall enter Heaven before the rich (Tirmidhi). What they should have received in this world was usurped by the greed of others, so they will be rewarded far greater in the after-life. What can be said of a world in which individuals exist who would need multiple lifetimes to spend their wealth entirely, and people dying of starvation in the same place?

But since there is this culture of selfishness and greed, don't take my word for it when I say it is wrong. Sharing is a necessary quality for basic survival at the simplest form of civilization. Ibn Khaldun mentions in his famous work "The Muqaddimah" that the philosophers expressed: 'Man is "political" by nature. That is, he cannot do without the social organization for which the philosophers use the technical term 'town' (polis)'. He continues to say how this necessary character of sharing/social cooperation is explained by the fact that 'God created and fashioned man in a form that can live and subsist only with the help of food…' However, one person alone hasn't the power to provide enough even for himself. 'Even if we assume an absolute minimum of food – that is, food enough for one day, (a little) wheat, for instance – that amount of food could be obtained only after much preparation such as grinding, kneading, and baking. Each of these three operations requires utensils and tools that can be provided only with the help of several crafts, such as the crafts of the blacksmith, the carpenter, and the potter.' Put simply: if you want to live, you must share. If cooperation is needed at such a base level, this sentiment should permeate even stronger once society reaches the extent we see today. Instead, we regress, taking advantage of the fact that there are so many people and so many things, thinking that being greedy here and there won't cause much of a mess because the world is too big. Yet now whole systems are built upon exploiting rather than supporting. All it takes is one bit of ice to fall to start an avalanche…

To earn in a positive manner, you need an education of some sort. A farmer learns how to grow and tend crops, and the etiquettes of trade. A doctor will earn after having studied medicine. Education covers everything. Before doing anything, you need to learn. Your whole life is about constantly gathering knowledge of some sort. As I mentioned before, education is ultimately for the enhancement of our character. Obtaining wealth in a good way (which is what school is for, so it's not all bad!), and using it well, falls under this. Don't stop your learning and education at just getting money. It should continue to figuring out how to use it in a manner that uplifts those around you. Learn how and where to spend your money!

There'll still be room for you to buy many nice things, as well, so don't fret. As the famous hadith shows, the Prophet (peace be upon him) stated: "No one will enter Paradise who has an atom's weight of pride in his heart.' A man asked: 'What if a man likes his clothes to look good and his shoes to look good?' The Prophet (peace be upon him) replied: 'Allah is beautiful and loves beauty. Pride means denying the truth and looking down on people (Sahih Muslim).'" So, wear your designer clothes, and dress well! Just make sure you're clothing the poor and needy, too. My friends know that I'd be wearing Yeezy shoes right now had I the expenses ha-ha. But at the same time, I'd (hopefully!) be looking for ways to use my wealth to improve my community. Indeed, the Qur'an states: "And abundantly proclaim the favours of your Lord" (Qur'an, 93:11). If Allah has blessed you with wealth, then buy your nice clothes with the intention of showing the blessings Allah has bestowed upon you, for He loves this act (and so do you – who doesn't like wearing nice clothes?). But bear in mind the previous verse: "And do not rebuke the beggar" (Qur'an, 93:10).

One thing that particularly saddens me is when I look to the example(s) that I was raised to always look to, call to and emulate by my family and by my teachers: that is of the Ahlul Bayt (the Household of the Prophet peace be upon him). Every narration I hear speaks of their simplicity and their immense generosity. They only gained in order to give away – completely. They gave to such an extent that it left them without food and wealth. And they are the successful ones. What saddens me is that if we go in accordance with current ideas of success, would they be looked at as failures if they were here today by some Muslims? Of course not, for God wouldn't allow for such a thing. God has placed in the heart of the believers love for these pure people. Yet we have strayed from their example…

"I am leaving among you that which, if you hold fast to it, you will never go astray after I am gone, and one of the two is greater than the other: the Book of Allah, which is a rope extended from heaven to earth, and my family, the people of my household (ahl bayti). These two will never be separated until they come to me at the Cistern, so watch how you deal with them after I am gone." (Tirmidhi)

I am also reminded of the narration regarding Abu Bakr as-Siddeeq, the Greatest Companion: Umar ibn al-Khattab reported: 'The Messenger of Allah, peace and blessings be upon him, ordered us to give charity and at the time I had some wealth. I said to myself, "Today I will outdo Abu Bakr, if ever there were a day to outdo him." I went with half of my wealth to the Prophet and he said, "What have you left for your family?" I said, "The same amount." Then, Abu Bakr came with everything he had. The Prophet said, "O Abu Bakr, what have you left for your family?" Abu Bakr said, "Allah and his messenger." I said, "By Allah, I will never do better than Abu Bakr."' (Tirmidhi)

CHAPTER 2: WEALTH

What more needs to be said in regards to wealth and our attitude towards it?

7

Poem 2: Sky and Coast

I am caught up in two separate worlds
And am I slowly losing sight of both?
I am told that both these worlds clash with swords.
Will I be destroyed joining sky with coast?

This conundrum rings silently and deep
And it does not seem to be bothersome.
Yet one shout can cause a cattle stampede -
I fear that it may become cumbersome.

I live in this world, but aim for the next,
And it's beautiful here, but greater awaits.
Ignore my love in East, for what lies West?
Solved, or another problem it creates?

Then I laugh at such a silly trouble
For God has Mercy, and loves the humble.

8

Chapter 3: Friendship

A true friend is something becoming more and more scarce. Just speak to your grandparents if you don't believe me. Ask them about their friendships and compare it to the friendships of today.

You can't expect to be a good friend if you don't know what being a friend means. Similarly, you can't expect your 'friend' to be a real friend if he/she doesn't know what comes along with the title.

Friendship is more than knowing someone for a long time. It is more than having a laugh and a joke with someone. Friendship today has seemingly been limited to the people we go out and have fun with. It's no wonder why so many people feel so lonely. Real friendship is a helping hand to pull your friend out of the abyss. There's going to be highs and lows, ups and downs. Don't say you are close with someone, or that you're someone's friend, if you are only willing to stick by them when it's easy. Don't say you care or love someone, and when that person does something wrong, or faces disgrace, or is left in despair, you're going to leave them. Otherwise, you're a liar. You're not willing to stick by him/her because you fear people will think bad of you, or because it makes your life a little bit harder? Your company is irrelevant then. Life is a journey at sea; there will be easy sailing at times, but also storms before you reach your destination. A friend is there to help you navigate through the storm. If all the sailors (friends) jump ship, then the chances of crashing are higher. Friends are here to provide good times, and help you climb out of bad times.

Just like a husband or a wife should never dishonour the vow of marriage, a friend should remain faithful. However, mistakes are going to be made; your friend will forget your birthday, they will not be able to make it out for every plan, they will hurt your feelings by making fun of you, they will do things that make you angry, they will do things that disappoint you; the job of a friend is to remain loyal through all of this, and help their friend rise above. Friendships are such failures now because they don't fulfil their purpose, which is to support one another. If your friend does something wrong, your job is to help them realise their mistake and guide them through. You don't just cut them off and move on. You should never have spent time with them in the first place, then. When you make a decision or do something, there are consequences to that. You have to accept and deal with them, good or bad.

CHAPTER 3: FRIENDSHIP

Don't anticipate your friends slipping up. Don't wait for an opportunity to cut them off as soon as they make a mistake. What kind of friendship is that then? Usually, it is an enemy who waits for a person to fall.

Relationships are about accepting people despite their shortcomings. Something that upsets you may seem like nothing to your friend; that's no reason to cut them off – purely because they aren't wired the same as you. If you can't deal with difference, then befriend those who are exactly the same as you... which is virtually impossible. Don't complain then, however, of boredom.

There are limits nonetheless. Certain things shouldn't be excused unless one wishes to be made a fool of. Question and warn your friend if they sit comfortably with your enemy, for example. Just a little side point: your enemy isn't the person you get into a fight with over petty matters like trying to solve who is stronger, or whatever. An enemy is someone or something hoping for your downfall. Don't break your principles for your friends, either. They should respect your values even if they disagree with them. Right and wrong doesn't change for anyone.

There are many layers to companionship. It isn't just who is in-front of your face. It is who remembers you when you're not with them - and most importantly, who speaks to God about you. It is who would look out for your mother when you aren't around, who would watch out for your siblings the way you would watch out for your own. Friendship in the truest form is family. Only a few people in your life will ever achieve this rank of closeness. You can have many friends, who all genuinely care for you, but you will only ever have a handful of people who can be regarded as family. Each relationship must be given its due in accordance to its rank.

Therefore, to determine who your friend is takes time - many, many years. At the moment, you and those who you keep company with are in the process of attaining friendship. That's the target you are supposed to have in mind as you spend time and develop relationships with people. Sitting with a person doesn't make them a companion. You will grow together, go through different situations, face adversities, experience joys, create memories and go through life. Some people will remain with you till you die, passing the majority if not all the tests of friendship. Some will pass many, but eventually fail or have to separate because their path of life leads elsewhere. That's okay. That isn't a reason to hate the person, bare grudges or anything of the sort. Instead, honour that person and yourself by parting ways with dignity, for despite the shortcoming and failure in attaining the rank of friendship with you, the person passed a lot more tests than failed. Their friendship may be fulfilled with someone else. Humans have a bad habit of forgetting a lot of the good a person has done whilst latching onto the mistakes. Such negativity is what ultimately holds us down.

Your friend, to give some pointers, shouldn't be a yes-man/woman. Your friend isn't the person who is always complimenting you and feeding your ego – that is nothing but a devil in disguise. Instead, it is someone who wants you to improve. At the same time, someone who fails to appreciate the good qualities you possess is troublesome. Too many people surround themselves with individuals who do nothing but feed each other's egos and live in their own bubble, unaware of reality. Of course, it isn't in everyone's nature to provide tough-love. Some people are very soft, and both qualities have their merits. But where there is something wrong, acknowledge it is wrong – whether in a friend or family member or a stranger.

At the end of it all, sometimes it is simply a matter of hearts; of souls. You will feel unique connections with certain individuals that seems distinct from other friendships. These are the people you need to discern and actively seek to remain with. Kindred spirits. It can be one person, or a couple, but no more than a handful. Such friendships are truly beautiful. Regardless of how long you're separated, as soon as you reunite you pick up immediately from where you left of. This is because such friends think only well of you. They think of you in a positive light, and the distance and separation doesn't allow for doubts to creep in, or negative opinions to develop. This is God's protection; God's blessing.

Mawlana Rumi states that if you're expecting a faultless friend, you will be left alone. Humans are fallible. Do not put a standard of perfection upon your friends. That only makes you a bad one. Be open hearted and easy going. And the relationship you should think about cultivating as a priority, more so than all others, is your connection with God. Make God your guardian, and friend. "I am as my servant thinks I am." (Hadith Qudsi) There is no relationship more important, beneficial, beautiful and necessary than this one. God is the only Friend that will be with you even when you have nobody else. Our first port of call at every instance should be our Lord.

Keeping good company is vital. The Prophet, peace and blessings be upon him, said, "Verily, the parable of good company and a bad company is only that of a seller of musk and a blacksmith. The seller of musk will give you some perfume, you will buy some, or you will notice a good smell. As for the blacksmith, he will burn your clothes or you will notice a bad smell." (Bukhari and Muslim) Ultimately, we should seek to be around those who remind us of our Lord, and who are good people.

9

Poem 3: Pain is the Answer

My bed is 'struggle' and 'pain', my cover.
My heart is heavy, and body, sickly.
My head is in the clouds, eyes on Mother.
My desire is to end this cycle quickly.

"Aim for the next life", "this life is a test".
I try, but the pain remains and haunts me.
Am I at fault, my chest become a nest
For pain so that I weep and try to flee?

But Rumi tells that the pain is the door.
Medicine can poison – can poison heal?
In this pain lies the answer, lies the cure.
In this pain is the route to the warm feel.

The struggle is the path to God's nearness.
Work towards bliss, each step earning wellness.

10

Chapter 4: Happiness

This is the underlying goal that everyone seeks. The one who chases riches does so with the belief that therein lies his or her happiness, or whatever target an individual may be aiming for. Ultimately, we all just want to be happy.

The reality is that there can never be a true sense of happiness. At least not entirely. It can be experienced, like at the birth of a child, where the parents experience a happiness that is incomparable. That same child will grow to face a sadness that is incomparable when the parents die. Happiness and sadness are parts of the package that is this life. Ignoring one in favour of the other is destructive because you can't appreciate one without the other. You wouldn't know happiness unless you had experienced sadness; you won't understand sadness unless you feel bliss.

You can't allow yourself to succumb to the darkness of sadness.

Too long in the dark and you'll lose your sight. You also can't allow yourself to be drawn in senselessly by the light of happiness. If you look too long at its brightness, you lose sight of things around you and may lose your sight all-together – just like in the darkness. You may have noticed that I like my metaphors. What I'm basically pointing out here is that if you completely fall into your sadness, it'll take away much from you; physical well-being, mental well-being, your peace. Give sadness its time, but don't let it stay longer than it needs to. Similarly, don't jump head first into happiness. There's a reason our Prophet (peace be upon him) said to never make promises in states of extreme joy, because in such a state you're not aware of other parameters. You lose sight of all else; you forget your responsibilities, you forget pain, school, life in general (ha-ha). So, just like with sadness, give happiness it's time, but don't go to extremes - with anything, in-fact. There's a time and place for everything. It may be easier said than done. It's your job to figure out what helps you. Exercising, eating healthily, reciting the Qur'an regularly such things will help you regulate your states when they fluctuate, hence why the Sunnah prescribes these things for habitual application.

Rather than happiness, which is experienced in certain moments or events in life, our goal should be to attain contentment. Unlike happiness, which is fleeting, contentment is a state of mind and soul that can be trained and held onto throughout all avenues of life. I know before I said that to be wealthy is to be happy, but that means that wealth is also temporary, because happiness (as I have just explained) is temporary. I'd therefore say that the greatest wealth is contentment. Happiness is definitely a treasure. But it rusts. Contentment is a diamond that shines forever but be careful: you don't want to lose it.

This brings us to the matter of patience (sabr). I'd argue that patience is probably the greatest quality a person can have. To be patient in all states – when calamity hits, to be patient in happiness, also. It suffices to say that "indeed, Allah is with the patient" to show the beauty and importance of this quality. Life is difficult, but we have to be patient through whatever we face. As the statement attributed to the first Caliph of Islam, Abu Bakr as Siddiq (Allah be pleased with him), states: "It is difficult to be patient but to waste the rewards of patience is worse." Patience is being content with the will of Allah. It is facing a trial head on, accepting what has happened and moving forward to improve. Patience is the will to keep on going. It isn't sitting and waiting for things to get better. It's the complete opposite. Patience is not allowing a trial or a difficulty to put you down. Patience is strength. A hadith mentions: "I swear by Allah, I heard the Messenger of Allah (peace be upon him) say: The happy man is he who avoids dissensions: happy is the man who avoids dissensions; happy is the man who avoids dissensions: but how fine is the man who is afflicted and shows endurance." (Sunan Abu Dawood) How great is that man or woman who faces difficulty but is patient. Continues to strive.

Life will throw whatever it can at you to bring you to your knees. Try your best not to let it. Or, at least, go down with a fight. The greatest champions are those who face the greatest opponents, no? Even if they lose, they're given glory. Nobody

CHAPTER 4: HAPPINESS

wants to be weak. To be strong, however, requires hard work and pain. You have to bear on and endure. What other choice is there, anyway, when weakness promises nothing but pain and suffering, also? As the famous quote attributed to Tipu Sultan famously said: "It is better to live like a lion for a day than to live like a jackal for a hundred years."

Travel around and you may come across some poor people who will greet you with a smile despite their destitute condition. It's not because they're happy necessarily, but it's because they're content. They're satisfied with whatever God wills for them/ have come to terms with their condition, whilst at the same time constantly seeking to improve their state. It's a delicate but beautiful balance. The living embodiment of poetry. As Maulana Rumi says: 'life is a balance of holding on and letting go'... Only then can one be content. What we, as individuals, need to do is spend time trying to unravel this statement. How can we achieve a balance of holding on, but letting go? I hope this book can provide some guidance (and ultimately all guidance is from Allah Almighty) in this, but at the end of the day, it's a journey that an individual must take. It's no fun if you just get given all of the answers, you have to experience for yourself ha-ha.

You must pick what you care about, and make sure they are things that are worth your time and effort. How can you evaluate this? It's that which gives your spirit peace, which is achieved through building Taqwa (awareness of God). Go after your passion, what you were made to do. Therein lies your success and peace. Honour your family ties as much as possible, for family is power. It's a support system, a home, a place of recluse and your allies. Honour your friendships because they are your other family. Understanding this will help you understand a lot of other things. As Rumi says: "set your life on fire", with your passion, with your love of goodness, and "seek those who fan your flames."

It's an oft quoted sentiment that the happiest people are those who give the most. Those who do the most for others without expecting anything in return. Those who sacrifice. Those who are selfless. Realistically, this isn't for everyone. Not everyone can sacrifice massively for the greater good. But do what you can. Give as much as you are able to give. Money, time, love, words, hugs, respect, honour. Give as much of these things as you can to those deserving of it, and you'll not only get more of it back, but you'll feel good about it. Develop a habit of giving without expecting anything in return, for this is the real kindness, and God grants the rewards for such acts (and something from God is better than being given something from a human). Start small: when you're walking home from school and buy yourself a chocolate bar, give a piece to all your friends who walk with you, even if it means you have none left at the end.

Your job is to morph into what you are capable of becoming, based on whatever skills, intelligence, physical strength and heart you have. If you enjoy and are good at maths, don't try becoming a boxer. Follow your strengths and heart, and you'll

CHAPTER 4: HAPPINESS

excel. Don't try to fit into something you're not meant for. You'll be a bigger help to yourself, those around you and to society at large working to your strengths.

Plan in accordance to your capabilities. Look at your abilities, your resources and environment and do the most you possibly can with what you have available. All of these things play a part. Success isn't just becoming a CEO. Success is achieving the best you can with what you have to work with. Intelligence shouldn't simply be praised for intelligence's sake. It's a praise-worthy quality only when used properly - a smart, but lazy person isn't praiseworthy, but a waste of potential, is it not? Intelligence is also something very broad. It isn't restricted to doctors and lawyers. A doctor doesn't know how to build a house, yet his intelligence is extremely praise-worthy whereas the builder is looked down upon in comparison, for whatever reason. There are different types of skills, works and so on that require different minds.

If a person's potential extends to the level of becoming a waiter, or a labourer, and they work hard, they are successful. They are earning money by playing a part in society, feeding themselves and family. That deserves respect. The one who does well in school because of the intelligence he/she is blessed with, and then uses that intelligence, rather than wasting it, to become an engineer or doctor also deserves respect. With a mindset like this, you'll aim for your best, while at the same time remaining down to earth and humble because you'll realise that you're no better than anyone due to your big job role. Why? You were able to reach that, so you should have - through hard work and effort, no doubt. The waiter – that was his or her best. They had to put the same effort as the doctor, relatively, to reach their role based on their abilities and circumstances. Some of the smartest and most intelligent people I have met were working in factories. They didn't end up there because they didn't try hard. It's just a matter of circumstance and opportunity. It's the people of humility who are the most content. As long as a person constantly strives to improve, they are successful regardless of where they reach or don't reach. Just never become complacent. When you look at the bigger picture, a job role is just a piece of the puzzle.

Imam Ghazali, who was the Head of prestigious educational institutes of his time, chose to become a cleaner in a mosque when he became older (and wiser/more intelligent). That's something interesting to think about...

Keep this in mind, too: everyone has a role to play. Imagine if everyone was a doctor. Who'd build the hospitals? Now you need builders and architects. Who's going to make the equipment for the doctors? Now we need engineers. Who's going to log all the information about the patients? We now need admin staff. Who's going to ensure everything is clean to make sure disease doesn't spread within the hospital? You now need cleaners. Everyone is required. As Mufasa mentions in The Lion King, "it's the circle of life" ha-ha. If there weren't any binmen, your streets after a few months would be full of rubbish. You wouldn't be able to drive to the job that makes you so arrogant... So don't get big headed because of a job role, and don't feel low due to one, either. Respect is based on character. How you carry yourself. That is what differentiates who is 'better' or 'superior', as mentioned in the statement of the Prophet (peace be upon him) in the opening of this book.

What you may begin to notice is that all the different things explained so far are all tied together. If you're missing one, you're missing a big part of the other. You need each in proportion to get the most out of them all. I'll show you why: you may have come across the saying 'ignorance is bliss'. This saying has truth in it. Children are usually the happiest of all. They're also completely naïve. They don't know anything about the world until they become adults. But in order to fully appreciate bliss and happiness, you need knowledge of what it is you're experiencing, and also to experience the opposite (sadness). This is why we only really appreciate our childhood in retrospect, and why nostalgia is a thing. We therefore need education to understand what we are feeling and experiencing. Yet it's also known that those who learn the most about the world, and life, usually fall into sadness from learning of the terrible things that happen all the time. This is becoming more educated, but at the expense of our happiness. However, in this situation a person may have friends who make them smile, feel warm and happy again. In order to know about who those real friends are and to protect oneself from bad company that will only cause loss, education/knowledge is once again a necessity. I'm sure you get the picture. They're all linked in some way.

"Verily, in the Remembrance of Allah do hearts find peace" (Qur'an, 13:28). As mentioned before, your money, friends, cars, houses, family, jobs (you name it) will only bring you true peace when they are linked to your purpose. And that is to Remember God. Earning millions won't bring you peace; earning millions to help God's creation will bring you peace, however. Therein lies the distinction. And there's still room to spend on and enjoy yourself, for God is Merciful. The Prophet peace be upon him said: "Religion is easy, and no one overburdens himself in his religion but he will be unable to continue in that way. So do not be extremists, but try to be near perfection and receive the good tidings that you will be rewarded. Gain strength by worshipping in the mornings and afternoons and during the last hours of the night" (Bukhari).

Poem 4: Life is a Melody

Life is a melody, a song, and I
Wish to dance all the way till the grave's long
Embrace. There are low notes, and high notes. Why?
Well, it adds to the beauty of the song.

Isn't it strange to lay down when song plays?
So what if it's sad? I'll dance with a frown
And when happy, I'll smile the sun away.
Sadness, a sea. Dance on water, don't drown.

I want to go to the grave an artist.
My dance will be my masterpiece to show.
Hear the beat, and dance all day – the heart-is-
Strong! Open your ears; harmony will flow.

The heart beats, so there's a beat to dance to
Art is movement, as is life. So move, too!

12

Chapter 5: Discipline

Self-control is very important. This is something I myself am trying to improve on. If you are not able to control your emotions, your anger, your sadness, your desires and your wants, you will be controlled by others easily. You are easily manipulated. You are vulnerable. And in the world that we live in today, there aren't many protectors of the vulnerable, seemingly… You are also more susceptible to Devilish influence. Islam has a big focus on discipline for a reason.

Do not allow others to dictate your feelings so easily. Learn to understand what type of reaction is needed for a given situation. Learn what type of emotions work best at different times. Most importantly, learn not to open yourself up. Do not trust anyone. Especially with yourself. Not everyone deserves to know you. Learn to keep people at an arm's length. Only have in an embrace those who love you. Be warm and well-mannered, but don't leave your door wide open and then complain about being robbed.

From my experience, and from hearing of the experiences of others and learning from their mistakes, it is best to keep yourself reserved and to yourself. Something that bugs me quite a lot is needless talk. I find that so many people speak purely for the sake of saying something. They'll have nothing beneficial to say, but will just feel the need to speak nonsense. This is a waste of time and effort, and it conditions your mind to nonsense. When all you're used to is idle chatter, your brain won't be prepared for fruitful speech. Avoid this as best as you can. Don't be rude. But don't allow anyone to waste your time. What you make habitual is what you're programming your brain to take in. My dad reminds me and my siblings about the danger of speaking too much, and the importance of listening deeply. He would say that the one who talks a lot usually ends up revealing more than he/she even wanted, making a fool of themselves eventually. They're also not taken very seriously in the long run. As the Prophet (peace be upon him) stated: "speak good or remain silent" (Bukhari and Muslim) and to speak good is to mention Allah and avoid speaking a lot without God's remembrance for this makes the heart become hard and distanced from God (Tirmidhi). Indeed, the Prophet (peace be upon him) said that most of the sins of people are on the tongues (Mu'jam al Kabir).

Don't get me wrong, you can speak about football, the weather, your favourite colour and so on. There's no harm in it. Infact, these things bring us closer to one another, which is praiseworthy (if done with that intention for the right people). Just don't only talk about that.

Being able to admit your mistakes to yourselves and to others will get you far. Don't be afraid of this or feel that it somehow lowers your standing. You'll only learn if you make mistakes. When corrected, actually take the correction into account and think about it properly. Then apply it. If, after reflecting upon the advice or correction, you feel that in-fact you had made no mistake, there is no harm in seeking further explanation. And if, still, you feel you were not in the wrong, remember that life isn't just one small road. There's room for more than one correct way of handling things. Just because someone does something different, doesn't mean they're incorrect. What is incorrect, for Muslims, is that which contradicts the religion. That which is forbidden is what has to be avoided completely. Then there are different etiquettes and manners – not everyone is the same in this regard. Be humble enough to understand this. There is a general rule or principle that all must abide by. Within that, though, there is room for flexibility to account for different circumstances as well as different tendencies and characters. Open-mindedness is a very important trait to possess. You'll enjoy life more that way.

The Prophet (peace be upon him) stated that "difference of opinion is a blessing in my Nation," and the scholars mention this is in reference to secondary issues. A century or two later, the different schools of Fiqh (Islamic Jurisprudence) within Islam formed, the most prominent being the 4: Hanafi, Shafi'i, Maliki and Hanbali. Though the belief is the same, it should be an eye opener for us Muslims that Imams of these Schools of Thought, all great mountains of knowledge, differed on many points from what breaks the fast, to the times of prayer.

The wisdom in this? Flexibility is a good thing. "O mankind, indeed We have created you from male and female and made you peoples and tribes that you may know one another. Indeed, the most noble of you in the sight of Allah is the most righteous of you. Indeed, Allah is Knowing and Acquainted" (Qur'an, 49:13). This isn't, however, some excuse to make play of the rules to find loopholes, unless one wishes to make a joke of the religion. The idea behind mentioning the 4 Schools of Thought is to take the lesson/wisdom of there being more than one approach to getting to the right answer as a general idea to one's approach to life. Where religion is concerned, caution is always the best approach.

You will come across many Ahadith mentioning the importance of controlling one's anger, controlling one's tongue, thinking of good thoughts and occupying the mind with knowledge and remembrance of God, controlling one's diet and so on. Fasting as a form of worship builds a lot of discipline in a person and is a pillar of Islam – this should tell us a lot of the importance of developing discipline and self-control.

With discipline comes the strength to fulfil one's duties. As I alluded to earlier, sometimes we will reach a crossroad where we have to choose between our duty and our desires/passion. Depending on the nature of the two, a person's choice will differ. Having a sense of duty and discipline, however, will ensure that the choice is always one that is dictated by what is right, which for Muslims is in light of God's commands.

God commands us to earn a living and provide for ourselves and our families. Therefore, I can't choose not to work because I don't like a job, while I wait for the job of my dreams. You have to be disciplined, and strong-willed, to work and do things even that you dislike, but in order to attain what you want in the long-run. Discipline allows one to focus on the bigger picture. I hated school and studying, but I hated the idea of being a failure much more; I hated the idea of not being able to provide adequately for my family in the future even more. So, I rolled with the blows, took some hits, but ultimately came out of the fight with a W. Now I am in a position where I can eventually work and do what I prefer. Had I avoided what I disliked, however, I'd be in a completely different place…

In order to summarise the importance of being disciplined, the following narration suffices: Ibn al-Mubarak reported: Hasan al-Basri, may Allah have mercy on him, said, "Verily, the believer is a guardian over himself and he holds himself accountable to Allah Almighty. The reckoning will only be lightened on the Day of Resurrection for people who held themselves accountable in this world. Verily, the reckoning will only be gruelling on the Day of Resurrection for people who did not hold themselves accountable." Be strict on yourself, and kind with others. But don't be a tyrant upon yourself.

13

Poem 5: Ambition

Action is always better than nothing
And I refuse to sit and wait, helpless.
The pain and anger aren't for moping.
They're for strength, and to become relentless.

I build, and break, and build again stronger.
The struggles continue without end, till death.
Call it madness: you'll learn to be fonder
Of trials; it is greatness being felt.

Ships to traverse these seas are not wanted.
I will dissolve them with my ambition,
Blazing inside to keep my heart mounted
On steed. Ride this storm to lands of fiction…

Call it anger, motivation, hunger,
My goal's simple: show God I'm a fighter.

14

Chapter 6: Manhood and Womanhood

Society or culture doesn't define what it means to be a man or a woman. Yes, culture and environment will no doubt influence a person's outlook on these things, but these are in minor aspects. What makes a man isn't the colour or style of clothing he wears/doesn't wear, as long as it is in accordance to what Islam stipulates, which is to have at least covered the navel to just below the knee in the Hanafi school, and not with tight clothing. Nor does wearing a certain colour or style take away from his manhood. If you want to know what a real man is in the most complete and perfect way, look at the Prophet Muhammad, peace be upon him, his Companions and the other Prophet's. They were real men.

The Prophet peace be upon him was kind, generous, soft-hearted, would cry often to God, loved his wives, loved animals and looked after the environment. He was incredibly shy, was the peak of humility and would make children happy. At the same time, he was the most courageous and most powerful (physically, mentally and spiritually), the wisest, the foremost in knowledge, the best keeper of his friends, the most honourable even to his enemies to the extent that they had to praise him, and I can go on. The Prophet peace be upon him embodied every quality of a man, and indeed a human being, in the most perfect way.

Our aim should be to try and gain whatever qualities we can, and perfect them. These can be gained by simply avoiding their opposites. Of-course, we are imperfect – but that doesn't mean we should be harmful. Making mistakes is excusable, but being irresponsible and dangerous is a different story.

Just because you're physically very strong and can fight, that doesn't make you any more of a man than the one who is, for example, physically weak but is good to his mother. If anything, the latter is a greater man for his action pleases God more. And that's what it all boils down to. Being a man means being of service to those you love, and those who love you. How you serve depends on what qualities and skills you possess. The greatest men are those who serve humanity. The Prophet (peace and blessings be upon him) said, "The nobility of a man is in his religion, his manhood is in his intellect, and his honour is in his character." (Ahmed) Why intellect in particular? Because through intellect, one can help and serve many.

A man isn't the one who is loud; a man isn't the one who is quiet. Everyone has their own personality which should be embraced.

Don't feel the need to change unless your personality traits are harmful to yourself and to others and contradictory to Islamic teachings. Be yourself. If you don't like who you are, if you don't respect yourself, don't expect others to. Your family and friends, however, love you as you are – even if you aren't the biggest fan of your personality. That should be reason enough to be happy with yourself. If they can accept you, you should, too. More importantly, God and the Prophet (peace be upon him) love you.

Overpowering, belittling, controlling, manipulating, abusing or bullying anyone aren't attributes of manhood. Especially if done to a woman. You're a man when you're fulfilling your duty, which is to serve your mothers, protect and care for your sisters, and be loyal and good to your wives. The Messenger of Allah (peace and blessings be upon him) said, "The most complete of believers in faith are those with the best character, and the best of you are the best in behaviour to their women." (Tirmidhi)

You're a man when you're honouring your friendships, family-ties and not being an idiot. To make it easy, find out what God asks of a man. What does God say makes a man? Society's definitions of manhood/womanhood, right and wrong are always changing. If you follow that, your opinion on right and wrong will clash with what your children in future believe to be right and wrong – and good luck keeping a family together in such an environment. "I like not those that set/disappear", as is mentioned in the story of Ibrahim peace be upon him in the Qur'an (Qur'an, 6:76). Consistency in certain things is necessary, otherwise it only brings about problems.

I mentioned earlier the issue of clothing, as well. It is a weird one, because I think culture plays a big role in this. Islam has a clear paradigm that men are not to imitate women and vice versa, including in regards to dress. Interestingly, however, what one culture considers to be the dress of men is considered more like the dress of women in another. For example, the thobe and shalwar kameez of the Middle Eastern and South East Asian cultures is more similar to the skirt worn by women in the West than it is to the clothing of men in the West. In fact, that skirt style of dress is seen all over the African and Asian continent. The reason why I mention this is because I have come across a strange irony amongst some Muslims in my town who, when seeing Muslim men/boys wearing Western style clothing that is very loose/over-sized (such as hoodies and cropped loose trousers) rather than tight t-shirts and slim-fit jeans that hug one's legs, they claim that that is feminine dress. The irony is that that type of dressing is closer to their parents' culture usually, and also closer to the Sunnah which is to wear loose, clean, presentable and modest clothing for men as well as women.

Womanhood, like manhood, shouldn't be based upon societal constructs. If you want to know what it means to be a woman, see what God has to say about it. Look up to the great women of history, the likes of Maryam (Mary), the Mother of Prophet Eesa (Jesus). May peace be upon them both. What you will notice is that God only lays down laws that both men and women must abide by for their own good. After that, there is a lot of room for all different types of personality types and characteristics. The "ideal" woman isn't the quiet, shy and agreeable female. And it isn't an independent, out-going type either. They're all fine. As long as you don't step over the boundaries laid out by God. And even when we do fall short in abiding the laws of God concerning dress, prayer and so forth, we find favour in the Mercy of God. What pleases Him the most is that we, men and women, try. Exertion. This is what matters.

You can learn a lot about a person through whom they look up to. If you're looking up to social media "influencers" and YouTube couples, you've sold yourself immensely short. This is something that really irks me. It's not a wonder we Muslims are in the state we're in when we're busy making role models out of such people. Appreciate and enjoy their content if you want, but don't make them into something they're not and aren't worthy of being and in some cases aren't even trying to be. Your role models have already been given to you. Women should be looking up to the likes of Rabia-al-Adawiyyah and Umm-ul-Khair Fatima, the mother of the King of Saints Shaykh Abdul Qadir Jilani, who sacrificed so much for her son to reach his rank. Men should be looking up to Sultan Salahuddin Ayyubi!

If we read our history, there is a rich tradition of women in scholarly positions, from teaching Qur'an, spirituality, to the preservation and narration of Ahadith. There is a book that we can all refer to, by Dr Mohammad Akram Nadwi, called "al-Muhaddithat: the women scholars in Islam." It outlines a long tradition of women scholarship in Islamic history going back to the Prophet's time, peace be upon him. Reading this, as well as furthering our research upon this topic, will dispel some misconceptions that exist around the role of women.

15

Poem 6: Love God

If there's no fire within, what's the use?
An oven can't cook without a hot flame…
You're afraid of burning? Here are some clues:
Hunger can kill; a burnt hand's pain will wane…

Living in fear is a poison that's slow.
A quick death is better than long torture…
Take risks! Failures, no matter how low,
Are to be embraced, for a strong future.

But rest assured, for I have sound advice,
A full-proof plan, that always yields profit:
Love God, and those God Loves, with all your life.
Give your heart – above all, to the Prophet.

Peace be upon him, the one with the smile
That makes all the pain and sorrow worthwhile.

16

Chapter 7: Arrogance

Arrogance isn't thinking you are special. Arrogance isn't acknowledging whether you are strong, or intelligent, or great at football. Arrogance can't be truthful. Being truthful is good, whereas being arrogant is bad, so the two can't go together otherwise it's a contradiction. Arrogance is a false sense of superiority for false reasons. 'Having or revealing an exaggerated sense of one's own importance or abilities', according to the online definition. My dad said this to me a while ago: "son, never look down on anyone, but don't look up to anyone either". Of course, we look up to our role models and those deserving of those stations, like our teachers and so on. But that is a general principle to live by so that you don't become arrogant, and so that you don't suffer from the arrogance of others.

There's a quote from one of my all-time favourite anime's, Fullmetal Alchemist Brotherhood, where the main character, Edward Elric, says: "even when our eyes are closed, there's a whole world out there that lives outside of ourselves and our dreams." You're important, but no more than every else. Be humble.

Your strength doesn't mean you're better than anyone. You're just stronger, not better. Your intelligence doesn't make you better than anyone. You're just smarter, not better. Your wealth doesn't mean you're better than anyone. You're just wealthier. Superiority is determined by one single factor: Taqwa. God consciousness. Use your strength with God in mind by defending the weak, and that is what makes someone better – not the strength itself. Use your intelligence to teach others, and you'll be a better person. Being just smart won't cut it. As the Prophet (peace be upon him) stated in his Farewell Sermon: "An Arab has no superiority over a non-Arab nor a non-Arab over an Arab; a white has no superiority over a black nor does a black have any superiority over a white except by piety and good action." Piety is what sets us apart. The scholars - who are the most pious - won't make anyone feel lower than them through their words or actions. They are welcoming to all, smiling and shining, and constantly tell themselves they are no better than any. If at any point you feel like you're better than the people around you for whatever reason, know you have gone wrong. A person who busies himself with his/her sins and shortcomings will not feel superior to any. Such a person will feel too shy and ashamed to possess such absurd self-perceptions.

Sometimes, though, there is a time to show people who and

what you are. Like on the football pitch.

Again, my aim is to only develop a spark, hopefully, because the enjoyment of thinking and pondering to figure something out and eventually reaching an answer is a fulfilling feeling. Being given answers is boring, and you're likely not to value them. So, think about this: you'll often find, especially in the Islamic Scholarly tradition, that the most wise and intelligent people are also the most humble, shy and down-to-earth. Why? They realised they only achieved what they were able to achieve based on the skill-set, tools and options made available to them in their lives and with God's grace, and rather than boasting about it, give constant thanks (to God) and show appreciation for it by helping others, smiling and being nice people.

Genghis Khan was one of the conquerors of the world, a military genius and terrifying individual who seemed to have imposed his will on the world. His name invokes terror due to how history remembers him. Yet, interestingly, Jack Weatherford in his work "Genghis Khan and the Making of the Modern World" mentions that he taught his sons "never to think of themselves as the strongest or smartest. Even the highest mountain had animals that step on it... when the animals climb to the top of the mountain, they are even higher than it is." "If you can't swallow your pride, you can't lead," he warned them. A valuable lesson to bear in mind.

17

Poem 7: Passage of Time

Oh, the waves of sadness that hit heart-ward,
Oh, the memories that destroy with smiles.
I am reduced to sighs and stares toward
The skies; this passage of time feels like knives.

So quickly it leaves us, sparing no one
A second glance. Nothing is as painful.
I wish to return to the days of fun,
The days of joy, when we were small, playful.

Yet you have to lose to appreciate.
What does a child know of the bliss of youth?
Time gives knowledge, and hope to replicate.
You'll live more aware of joy, that's the truth.

Live out your days with the smile of a child,
A warrior's heart, a spirit that's wild.

18

Chapter 8: Truth

This is what every one of us should be dedicating our lives to. The pursuit of truth is the very essence of life. All else is empty without the Truth being at the forefront. Ask, ask and ask again. Actively seek answers. Don't be passive. If you aren't worried about learning the truth, if you don't care for truth, be prepared to live a lie.

On the topic of lying, there is something very difficult we all must work on: don't tell lies. No matter how small. I once read that lying is for the scared, the cowardly: you only lie when you're afraid of the consequences. For example, when a child breaks something, and an adult asks if he/she is at fault, the child may place the blame elsewhere out of fear of being punished. Fear is what drives lies.

19

Poem 8: Fly or Fall

The confusion, the anger rages deep.
And as I feel it rising to the brim.
I envision, plan, and refuse to weep.
I pray that this isn't merely a whim.

I stand at the precipice – fly or fall.
Or can I turn and leave, back to comfort?
The thought crushes me, not meeting the call.
How can I turn on my heels, run-for-it?

This is the price for knowledge, my young friend.
A treasure requires excavation.
Gold must then be polished – it's not the end.
Worry? It promises gratification.

What choice do I have? Life's a death sentence.
Fly to Sun, die shining in elegance.

20

Chapter 9: Love

Love is sacrifice.
　Love is the greatest joy.
　Love is the greatest pain.
　Love is our purpose.
　Love is soft like petals.
　Love is tough like steel.

Everyone loves. But not everyone is a Lover.

21

Chapter 10: Parting Words

I don't want this to be too extensive. I wanted to outline a few important points that I feel people have come to misunderstand or not given due thought to, and describe them in a manner that is hopefully easily understood. More importantly, I want to encourage you to think. You may not get answers from reading this, but it will hopefully provoke some thought. That in itself is the answer. Once you take that first step in actually engaging your mind into the important things, the rest will follow at whatever pace is necessary. I hope you feel, as you read this, that it is like you are being spoken to by a worried friend who wants the best for you. From this point on, I'm just going to write whatever comes to my mind. I might put them into some order later on, or just leave them as they come along.

You not only owe it to the people who have sacrificed so much for you, but you owe it to yourself to be better, and to always try to be better. It pains me to see what my community is becoming, and I fear for what is to come. We need a complete

CHAPTER 10: PARTING WORDS

reform. We need a complete change of mindset. If we are to be a great people, which we once were and have the potential still to be, we need to go back to our roots. What do I mean by this? We need to value integrity. Honesty. Manners. Knowledge. Principles. Love. We will not find honour and success in trying to be like anyone else. We have to be ourselves – at an individual level, and as a collective people. Yes, we can learn from others, but you take what you learn and shape it around you. You don't assimilate and lose yourself. Keep the identity God gave you. One of the biggest problems people with a similar background as me are struggling with is an identity crisis. You are whatever God made you, and made you to become. Strive towards that.

You've been chasing all the money you could, working as many hours as possible, and your child still isn't well equipped for the world. Yes, I am talking to the parents here, should any be reading this. If not, I hope the child reading this will take it into his or her hands and pass on the message. Your money will not protect your child from the dangers of the streets. The hours you spend in your office will not protect your child at all. Safety is with God. No goodness nor harm can affect us except that it is the Will of God. If you desire goodness for your child, you need to spend time with them. You need to speak to and educate them. In order to do that, you yourself as a mother and father need to be educated about life and religion. Children now speak nicer to their friends than to their own parents – friends who have done absolutely nothing for them other than provide some laughs. The same parents who have done so much – without the child even knowing – can't even speak to their son or daughter. And you being at work 24/7 isn't going to mend that.

Worry about your relationship with your child more than how much pocket money you're giving them. A parent's role is to fulfil the needs of their offspring – financially, but more importantly, mentally and spiritually. A child's role is to be dutiful, respectful and once the parents have reached old age, to look after them the way they had looked after the child. As parents, the opinion your kids have of you is far more important than what people think of you. Rather than impressing outsiders who won't do anything for you, and will spit on you the first chance they get, impress your children. Once you die, it is your offspring who shall keep your name alive. They're your legacy. You'll be forgotten by everyone else. Don't risk being forgotten by your children, too. Be an active part of their lives as understanding, loving parents.

Our community should be flourishing with knowledge, wealth through hard work, and love. Instead, our community is filled with fakes, avarice, drugs and drug dealers, backwardness and people who don't mind their business. It's a real shame. Your children once they're older aren't going to be able to boast about their father's or mother's nice car for very long. But if their parents left behind a legacy of aid, and love and education, then that pride and boast will last several lifetimes. But no, we are far too small minded these days.

Our answers lie in the Qur'an and the Life of the Prophet peace

CHAPTER 10: PARTING WORDS

be upon him. There isn't a single question that we won't find the answer to in these places. If you want to see what real friendship is, look at the friendship between the Prophet peace be upon him and Abu Bakr as Siddeeq (may Allah be pleased with him). Uthman ibn Affan (may Allah be pleased with him) was one of the wealthiest men of his time, but look at how he used his wealth – today, over fourteen hundred years later we still speak of his great deeds! Umar ibn al-Khattab (may Allah be pleased with him) was a leader of all leaders, yet he wept constantly in worry, and roamed the streets at night looking for even an animal to feed that fell under his rule, lest he fail in his role and be held accountable. Compare that to the leaders of today. Ali ibn Abi Talib (may Allah ennoble his countenance) and Hamza ibn Abdul Mutallib (may Allah be pleased with him) were the greatest warriors, of immense strength, yet they used their strength in a beautiful way to fight against injustices, such that we speak of their strength fourteen hundred years later. They didn't intimidate others just to feel special. This is success. That is victory. Imagine the reward Allah has granted them. If you want to see a real community, look at Medina-tul-Munawwarah in the time of the Prophet (peace be upon him). Racism was removed; everyone received justice; the poor were well looked after (by the rich!); women were treated with honour and dignity. Reach them we may not (except on the Day of Judgement, God Willing!), but we can attempt to emulate them, at least. It's for our own good, anyway. We do not need to be looking in the West, east or anywhere to figure out how to live a good life. The answers lie in our Islamic heritage.

Find something you're willing to die for, and try your best to live and fight long enough to see it come to fruition. That's how you will live with strength and dignity. That's how you'll be inspired and also inspire. But you need to spend time finding that thing, and verifying whether it's worth it or not. Time is precious. Only spend it on things worth it. As Marcus Garvey, one of the leaders of the early movement in America for the uplifting of the black community before the Civil Rights Movement, stated: "The ends you serve that are selfish will take you no further than yourself but the ends you serve that are for all, in common, will take you into eternity."

End:

And so, this tangent comes to an end, finally. After dragging on, I would like to end it on this point: don't live for yourself, and don't live for others; live for a goal and you'll fulfil both. If you live just to chase your own desires, you'll lose those around you; live just to make others happy and you'll lose yourself. Live for a goal and you'll fulfil both. The bigger and purer the goal, the more of yourself and the more of others you'll attain; and there's nothing better than living for God and making it our aim to be obedient to Him. I believe in all earnestness that whatever has been written in this short work, if thought upon and implemented, can form a solid foundation in order to take life head on and fight. Because that's all we really need to do: fight to earn what we deserve. Fight for a better life. If not here, then definitely for the Next Life. Don't expect a better life to come to you. But always remember: you cannot make a better life for yourself at the expense of someone else's. You'll destroy your afterlife in doing so.

Ultimately, we are humans. We are imperfect, we are sinners. Our life is defined by our rising and falling. We shall achieve goodness, and fall into evil. So be easy on others, and be easy on yourself. In order to be content, you have to pursue goodness. Always try to sleep having done more good deeds than bad, and pray for forgiveness. We humans are weak, but are made strong by our Lord. The one advising is no better than the one being advised; both are equally capable of good and bad. Everyone makes mistakes. Accepting this quality in yourself and others is vital. Listen to what is being said, rather than looking at who is speaking, for goodness can come from anywhere – and guidance is from the Lord.

As Muslims, we have to try our best to uphold the Rights God has over us (Huqooq-Ullah) and the Right of the People (Huqooq-ul-'Ibaad). In regards to God's Rights, this is prayer, dressing in the prescribed manner, reciting the Qur'an etc. Indeed, we may fall short in these things. God is Merciful and will forgive you if you make up for missed prayers, for example, and attempt to improve in these things. However, what we must be especially careful of is the rights pertaining to the people. God will not forgive us if we harm another, except if they first forgive – and humans do not forgive and forget easily. This is why our manners and characters are what we must give just as much attention to. The purpose of all the prayers, Qur'an and sending Salutations (Darood) upon the Prophet (peace be upon him) is to improve our character! So that we may be kind to each other. This is what the test is. Indeed, the Prophet (peace be upon him) stated that on the Day of Judgement, when God shall weigh our good and bad deeds, "nothing shall be heavier upon the Mizaan (the scale) of a believer than good character. Verily, Allah hates the vulgar and obscene." (Tirmidhi)

All praise is due to Allah, the Lord of the Worlds, Who in His Mercy and Wisdom granted me the ability to write this, and endless peace and blessings be upon all His Prophets and Messengers, from Adam, to Nuh, to Ibrahim, to Musa and to Eesa, and to their Leader: Muhammad, all of whom gave the message of love, wisdom and submission to God, whose lives present a manual by which to live successfully. I pray God guides me, and you.

Books to read:

I leave you with a small list of books I feel every Muslim must have read before they reach 18 years old, the age where most will either being University or head into work-life directly. This reading task should begin at around the age of 13/14 in year 9, where one's understanding is at a better level. Within these 4 to 5 years, each book should be read thoroughly and completely and in this rough order:

CHAPTER 10: PARTING WORDS

1. The Lives of Man by Imam al Haddad
2. The Alchemy of Happiness by Imam Ghazali
3. The Autobiography of Malcolm X
4. 1984 by George Orwell
5. The Masnavi (Volume 1) by Rumi
6. The Seerah of the Prophet Muhammad peace be upon him should be read throughout and in between each book or listened to in the form of speeches etc.

I strongly believe these 6 will create a very solid foundation. You will have a greater understanding of your place and purpose, begin to see the world for what is really is, and build in yourself a thirst for knowledge so you will continue to read (God Willing). Make the intention, take the first step and God will do the rest if He Wills. "And verily my success is only by Allah" (Surah Hud, verse 88). If you are already in university or indeed beyond and haven't read these works, it's never too late to get to it. Recommend them and buy them for your younger siblings/cousins and so on and read with them. These books should be read while you sit and learn how to recite the Qur'an with Tajweed, basic Islamic Jurisprudence (Fiqh) from a teacher – about the 5 pillars and how to perform them properly – and the basics of Islamic Belief (Aqeedah) that is in accordance to the Qur'an and Sunnah.

22

Bibliography

Weatherford, Jack, *Genghis Khan and the Making of the Modern World* (New York, Broadway Books, 2004)

Khaldun, Ibn, Rosenthal, Franz, Dawood, N.J., Lawrence, Bruce B., *The Muqaddimah An Introduction to History The Classical Islamic History of the World* (New Jersey, Princeton University Press, 2015)

Al-Ghazali, Imam, Khalaf, Marwan, *Mukhtasar ihya ulum ad-din* (Lympia/Nikosia, Cyprus, Spohr Publishers Limited, 2014)

Rumi, Mojaddedi, Jawid, *The Masnavi Book One* (New York, Oxford University Press, 2008)

Al-Hujwiri, Bin Usman, Ali, Al-Azhari, Shah, Karam, Muhammad, Sheikh, Ahmed, Anis, *The Kashf Al Mahjub* (Lahore, Zia-ul-Quran Publications, 2012)

Banks, Coleman, Moyne, John, Arberry, A.J., Nicholson, Reynold, *Rumi Selected Poems* (England, Penguin Books, 2004)

Al-Ghazali, Field, Claud, *Al-Ghazzali The Alchemy of Happiness* (Azafran Books, 2016)

X, Malcolm, Haley, Alex, Younge, Gary, *The Autobiography of Malcolm X with the assistance of Alex Haley* (Penguin Books,

2007)

Garvey, Marcus, Blaisdell, Bob, Negri, Paul, Crawford, Thomas, *Selected Writings and Speeches of Marcus Garvey* (Dover Publications, Inc. 2004)

Orwell, George, Pynchon, Thomas, Davison, Peter, *Nineteen Eighty-Four* (Penguin Classics, 2000)

Printed in Great Britain
by Amazon